diff

diff

diff

diff

same

diff

same

diff

diff

same

same

diff

same

diff

diff

diff

diff

same

same

diff

diff

diff

same

same

same

diff

same

same

diff

diff

same

same

diff

diff

diff

same

diff

diff

diff

diff

diff

same

same

same

diff

same

diff

same

same

diff

same

diff

same

same

diff

diff

same

same

same

diff

same

same

same

diff

diff

same

diff

same

same

same
diff

SAME

DONATO MANCINI

DIFF

TALONBOOKS

bienvenue

ようこそ

добро пожаловать

willkommen

欢迎

bienvenido

benvenuti

स्वागत

환영

welkom

بك أهلا

hoşgeldiniz

καλωσορισατε

bem-vindo

¡ütz apetik!

fàilte

taåyaå yahi

הבא ברוך

tervetuloa

ᎣᏏᏲ

ласкаво просимо

selamat datang

ᒪ◁ᐧᐧ

e kipa mai

benvingut

راغل است شه

bi xêr hatî

yá'át'ééh

wilujeng sumping

ᑐᵃᔅᏞᔑᒋᘝ

sgę:nǫ' swagwe:gǫh!

hachinchokmataa?

boozhoo, niijii

wotziye

kúha?ahat

aanin

minatakushini

maṭoj-u

peehtikway

gila kas'la

welcome

salve

before i start i want to say you shouldn't blame yourself
there's no point in beating around the bush
there's something we need to talk about
this is the most difficult thing i've ever had to tell anyone
the longer i wait the harder it's going to be
it's best if we face this right now
what i'm about to tell you won't be easy to hear
i know this will hurt but it has to be said
i don't like being the bearer of bad news
please sit down, this could come as a shock
you knew this was coming, right?
i hope this won't be a complete surprise
hate to break it to you
please don't kill the messenger
i have some really bad news
how do i even say this
this is really really hard for me
there are no words for what i have to tell you
i can't go on lying anymore
you aren't going to like what i have to say

stuff like that
that type of thing
and stuff
everything like that
and everything else
all that crap
what have you
so on
the list is endless
yadda yadda
so forth
or whatnot
all the rest of it
whatever the fuck else
suchlike
you name it
take your pick
the whole nine yards
all such nonsense
something like that
and so on and so on
blah blah blah
and other fun stuff
whatever
you know what I mean
take your pick

TRIGGER
WARNING
SPOILER
ALERT

Resources should be used productively, in a cost-effective manner.

Nobody should be compelled.

The clock cannot be turned backwards.

We have to live in the present.

Present generations cannot be blamed for the mistakes of past generations.

Everybody should be treated equally.

Injustices should be righted.

We have free speech in this country.

No one should be told how to think or what to think.

Telling people which words they can or cannot use is censorship.

I am friends with an X person, therefore I can say whatever I want about X people.

I am not racist, I just don't approve of that behaviour.

I only meant it as a joke.

Political correctness has taken so much *fun* out of
the world.

If you move to a new country, you should absorb its customs
and values.

Minority opinion should not carry more weight than
majority opinion.

No group should be given unfair advantages.

The individual is the basis of human society.

Anyone could do their jobs, so why should we pay them more?

If you raise the minimum wage, everything will just become
more expensive.

Instead of complaining, you should try to improve
your life.

Poor people need to learn to budget.

No one who works hard should be poor.

Anyone can succeed if they don't give up.

I succeeded, why can't you?

If I don't do it, someone else will.

Social programs are costly.

The money has to come from somewhere.

Nations, like persons, have to live within their means.

You have to be practical.

If you don't like something, say it at the ballot box.

If you don't vote, you can't complain.

They criticize, but they don't have any solutions.

We get the system we deserve.

Aren't you glad you live in a country where you can express
your political opinions?

Would you prefer *totalitarianism*?

Elections tell us what the majority want.

How about a *heterosexual* pride day?

Love is an investment; invest wisely.

Without families there is no society.

If your mother had had an abortion, where would you be?

It's a slippery slope.

Careful you don't open the floodgates.

Parents have the right to decide what their children are exposed to.

Noisy demonstrations only alienate ordinary people.

There are many ways to get your point across.

You can express your political views without inconveniencing others.

The city belongs to everyone who lives here.

Everyone has the right to feel safe.

All lives matter.

Violence is harmful.

Unions breed corruption.

Competition encourages excellence.

People need incentives.

Freedom is the freedom to *choose*.

Freedom is a right.

The cage is already open; you only have to walk out.

BEHAVIOURAL
SELF-BLAME
CHARACTEROLOGICA
L SELF-BLAME
SUPERSTITIOUS SELF-
BLAME FATALISTIC
SELF-BLAME ECONO
MISTIC SELF-BLAME

don't
resist
so hard
you will
only
make it
hurt more.

Each woman received a ladleful.

Hand-made utensils (*author's drawing*): (a) bowl made from a turtle's shell, (b) spoon made from half a coconut, (c) cup made from a gourd, (d) lamp using coconut oil, (e) cooking stove made from scrap aluminum.

By this time we had all acquired soup containers — a round tin with two holes punched near the top through which a string or narrow piece of material or wire was threaded.

Not having any utensils, he fashioned a fork from one of the dog's ribs.

"This is good wire for spoons," she said. "Will you teach me how to make a spoon?"

I made a spoon from a piece of drainage pipe.

For a soup-dipper a piece of pail hoop was riveted to the side of a condensed milk can, the two rivets being cut from a copper cent with the chisel driven with the shoe hammer. For soup plates a canteen was melted apart and the two halves formed each a plate.

Then with an old razor-blade I carved myself a spoon from a piece of wood and was fully equipped to dine.

It is the noon meal, but the dinner does not look inviting: the pan is old and rusty; the smell of the soup excites suspicion. The greasy surface, dotted here and there with specks of vegetable, resembles a pool of stagnant water covered with green slime.

Right in front of me on the table sat a tub of this thin soup with a scoop hanging off the side.

The kitchen meals were skimpy and, more or less, the same every day: a watery soup made of rice or sweet potato, and sometimes a bit of chicken or beef in vegetable broth.

Each day they received a pound and a quarter of rye bread and a soup made from stale codfish with a little barley in it.

Two meals are served out daily, consisting of one piece of peculiarly constructed bread, and one ditto of indescribable salt, yellowish-coloured pork, or meat that has had its nutriment entirely boiled out of it.

Occasionally a mixture, designated as soup, is doled out in tin pots.

We had one slice of bread in the morning and at lunchtime a pot of soup which was more or less like water.

Twice a week oatmeal was served, and in the winter months it was a godsend, for it was the only food served hot. But as the warm weather approached, so did the oatmeal worms; and as they were very husky specimens, large and hairy, they had a tendency to stick in our throats.

Supper could be muskmelon, mung beans, soup of some kind, maybe a duck egg or sardines.

On Sundays we were given coconut milk with our meal — it was so delicious I could barely stand its taste.

Different soups, too, had their characteristics, fats making for the top of the pot, turnips for the bottom.

Whether, for example, one's soup was served from the top or the bottom of the pot could make a tremendous difference in caloric intake.

To get a more or less uniform consistency, the soup had to be stirred well clockwise with the ladle, which was made of a pint-and-a-half tin-can attached to a metre-long wooden stick. Then, with a swift reversal of the stirring direction, the server had to fill the ladle with liquid from the middle layer of the cauldron's contents.

Despite stirring, the heavier and thicker soup would always go to the bottom, along with any particles of fish or grain.

The soup on top was the thinnest and the least nourishing.

Some of the bowls had been filled while the stuff hadn't settled yet after the stirring, and others were duds.

At the bottom of the pot there was always a residue of thick stuff, and I received more because of where I had been.

One day, which I called peaday, I took the drawer of our doctor's chest and went to the galley, which was the cooking place, with my drawer for a soup dish. I held it under a large brass cock, the cook turned it. I received the allowance of my mess, and behold! Brown water, and fifteen floating peas — no peas on the bottom of my drawer, and this for six men's allowance for twenty-four hours. The peas were all in the bottom of the pot. Those left would, I suppose, be taken and sold.

When we did not have anything at all to eat, we talked about food.

Her focus was on the day-to-day issues such as how to get enough to survive.

Specifically, how could he convince the man who ladled out the soup to go to the bottom of the pot and give him some of the peas that could be found there instead of just skimming broth off the surface?

Everybody wanted the thick sludge from the bottom, not the thin watery stuff from the top.

We didn't know how to join a soup line. We — my two sisters and I — didn't see ourselves that way.

How to dodge beatings, kicks, and a multitude of other punishments? How to fight the intense winter cold, the lice, and the fleas? How to get our ladle of soup from the bottom where it was marginally more nourishing?

In fact, I became fascinated with the way various people in the room handled their soup. Some ate it very slowly, using a spoon and savouring every sip. Others drank it down almost at a gulp, then sat back watching eagerly to see if there was any left over, anxious to be there first.

Some remember the good luck of getting a bowl of soup from the bottom of the pot, others remember nearly starving.

This soup was from the bottom, and a most welcome addition to my diet.

But as I skimmed, beneath this appeared another layer, which, when removed, showed still another; and so on, until I had scraped to the bottom of the can, and the last of the insects went with the last of my soup. Every scoured-out pea (or bean) which found its way into the soup bore inside of its shell from ten to twenty of these hard-crusted little weevils.

Afterwards, I drank my soup without skimming. It was not that I hated the weevil less, but that I loved the soup more.

It was slim pickings. No rations yesterday.

I remember standing in line to get my bowl of soup, praying the ladle would be inserted down where the soup was thick.

One's place in the dinner line — or one's connection to the soup server — was crucial.

Those who were amongst the first to receive a spoonful from the surface of the pot found themselves with thinner soup. Towards the end of the distribution, the soup was thicker.

Skilful calculations would get results worthy to boast about: heavy, rich vegetable soup; chunks of potatoes or meat; and sweet tea. Indeed, it was a subject to dream about.

So we'd ask the woman who was ladling the soup into the buckets. (Everybody had to bring their own bucket to get soup.) She'd dip the greasy, watery stuff off the top. We'd ask her to please dip down to get some meat and potatoes from the bottom of the pot. But she wouldn't do it.

That's how we learned to cuss. We'd say: "Dip down. God
damn it, dip down."

I was there, standing in long lines with a tin cup hoping
and praying the pot didn't get empty or I didn't faint
before I got to the front of the line. If you did, you just
got shoved aside and passed over.

Naturally, people tried to hang towards the end of a row,
however impatient they were to get to the food.

Clever ones waited for the end to get the thicker soup,
which might have a piece of potato or even meat in it.

After a seemingly interminable time, I held out my chipped
enamel dish for the ration of rice and soggy vegetables.
To my horror, the dish was too small. The servers told me
to return later for the remainder of my share. Precious
liquid off the vegetables leaked out the hole in the bottom
of the dish. Quickly I ate the meal and hurried back for
more, but the food servers only shrugged sympathetically
and pointed to the empty drums.

By now, food was in short supply.

With winter in full fury, there is little to eat besides bug-infested rice and rotten fish scraps.

Almost all of the horses had been eaten.

Molasses was substituted in place of our meat ration; a very poor substitute for these hungry skeletons.

More and more we stole from one another. Bread thefts became common.

Each became the merciless competitor of all the others as he jockeyed in line to get his bowl of soup from the bottom, rather than from the top, of the vat.

Women in soup queues fought over the last helpings at the bottom of the pot, where the greasy dumplings lurked. I had to wait in line in fifty or sixty below zero weather to get this precious food. Many times I was simply pushed out of line and had to go back to the end. When I got to the kitchen, the cooks announced they had no more soup for us until tomorrow.

The task of ladling out the broth from the huge steaming cauldrons was assigned on a rotation basis.

One piece of thread, a spoon, or an extra shirt meant a significant increase in wealth and status.

For an item of barter or extra food, we might fashion a needle from bone and offer to sew clothing. Many engaged in making jewellery out of trash.

A few, like him, got to wear an overseer's hat. It gave the wearer certain privileges, such as soup from the bottom of the pot, and it generally opened doors.

When I lined up for a meal, I was always very hungry. As my turn approached, I would concentrate all my mental energies on the person distributing the food, in an attempt to mesmerize that person into scooping down where the precious, more nourishing solids usually settled. I sometimes got the impression that this technique worked, although what undoubtedly worked better was being on friendly terms with whoever was holding the ladle.

If they liked you, you got your soup from the bottom of the pot, where all the good stuff rested. If they didn't like you, you ate nothing but broth.

Only favourites were given a scoop from the bottom of the pot.

With my work, I had purchased the good will of the beast. At night, when handing out our supper, she always dipped the soup spoon down where the soup was a bit thicker.

As an additional payment for my services, I could be sure that as long as soup was being dealt out at lunchtime, when my turn came he would dip the ladle right to the bottom and fish out a few peas.

The two cigarettes I received on Sundays, I would exchange for more bread.

More or less I was holding on, although I always felt hungry.

She scraped the bottom and showed us the empty cauldron. Nothing was left. There were no seconds.

Thieves were again at work, leaving many men without cups for their soup. As a result, many received their rations in their shoes.

Back then, too, selection determined who lived and who died: who got the job at the public works, who got a place in the workhouse, who got a full pint of soup.

Standard rations were distributed in front of everybody, so all could see who was given preferential treatment and who was discriminated against — who got nothing but a thin, watery soup, and who was given scraps of turnip scraped from the coveted bottom of the pot.

Certain people were accused of monopolizing kitchen duties, serving their compatriots from the bottom of the pot, while others were given greasy liquid scooped from the top.

She carefully served the soup into metal bowls, which were stacked behind her on the ground. This was a moment of glory and absolute power for her. She enjoyed every minute, lording it over her subordinates. All eyes looked at her ladle as she slowly picked up floating pieces of vegetable for her friends and favourites.

In the second year a soup cauldron arrived in this destitute place. Bones were boiled in it to make the broth. Two local men looked after the big pot and distributed the soup. It is said that they gave the first and thinnest part of the gruel to the people, while they kept the thicker part at the bottom for themselves.

The ones who dish out the food have been given this special privilege, often because they have paid bribes. Sometimes they skim the oil off of the curry. This means that the curry given to most has no flavouring or oil. Also, they sometimes allow the soya beans and other ingredients to sink. Then they filter out all these bulky food particles, which can be sold to anyone who can pay with cheroots, a precious trade item.

As kitchen aides, we always had to make sure we didn't stir
the contents too much, so most of the meat would remain
in the bottom of the pot. If we could keep it down, we
would be able to serve it to one of our friends when she
came along to get her portion.

Each woman in complete silence, naked, with outstretched
hands, accepted a dipper of tasteless and watery vegetable
soup.

Once, when I was ladling out watered-down soup, an old man
begged me for some vegetables from the bottom of the pot.
When I looked up, I recognized my own grandfather.

The soup they made from the old bones was so acid, it
burned their mouths.

Many years later, she would tell her children about those
difficult days: how she would crawl on the floor searching
for one tiny crumb that had been overlooked.

The new slogan became: "No Work = No Eat."

When one's life is reduced to this, how can it possibly have any meaning?

At the work site, we were brought lunch, and it happened that as you were eating the mosquitoes would fill up the bowl like buckwheat porridge. They filled up your eyes, your nose and throat, and the taste of them was sweet, like blood.

A ration of a teaspoonful of soft soap was distributed. Nobody knew what to do with it.

And then, again, the usual things happen: we all run to the hut, and we queue up with our bowls ready and we all have an animal hurry to swell our bellies with the warm stew, but no one wants to be first, as the first person receives the most liquid ration.

As usual, he mocks and insults us for our voracity and takes care not to stir the pot, as the bottom notoriously belongs to him.

I see so many just refuse to eat. They just sit down and die. I try bribery on them, offering cigarettes for each bite they take. It is a losing battle for most.

There are people who are said to have gone grey overnight. Are they the ones who have descended to the very bottom?

"Don't you like thick soup from the bottom of the pot?" she whispered.

At the same time he, like the rest of us, learned how precious it is to get soup from the bottom of the pot.

She said: You must learn where to stand in line so as to get the most nutrients.

Will you never learn? You know damn well it's better to lag behind; the best of the soup is on the bottom of the pot.

Never drink the water, which carries typhus. Never queue first for soup.

We had learned to get along without knives and forks, and we had long since learned to slurp our food without a spoon; neither the soup nor the porridge were ever thick enough to require a spoon.

Some had only tin cans to eat from — soup or bean cans, mostly — their rough-cut openings hammered carefully smooth with rocks so they could drink without gashing their lips.

After a few weeks, I learned to time my position in line.

I learned then what it's like to live on one bowl of transparent watery soup a day, carrying heavy stones and hewing wood, and to be treated like something less than dirt.

Everyone learned the old trick of running your finger around the inside of the tureen when the soup is gone, swabbing up the last precious drops and licking it dry.

We learned the value of food.

We, too, know that it is not the same thing to be given a ladleful of soup from the top or the bottom of the pot, and we are already able to judge, according to the capacity of the various pots, what is the most suitable place in the queue when we line up.

SECRETED

SECRETED

UNPACKABLE

UNPACKABLE

more

or

more or less

more or less more less or

more less or more less or more or less

more less or more less or more less or more less or

or more less less or more less more or more or less more or less

or more less less or more more less or more less or more less less or more or

less or more more less or less or more or less less or more more

less more or more less or less more or less or more

or more or less or less more more less

or less more more less or

less or more

more

less

or

more

or less or

less or more or more less

less more less more more more less more or

more or more less or less or more more less or less

more more more or less less or less less more less less less more or

or more less more or less less more more more more or less or more or more or

or more or more or more or more or more more more or less less

more less less or less more or less less less more less

less or more less or less or less more

or more less or less or

or more more

more

more

less

more

more more or

more more or less less or

less or less or more more less more more

more or more or less more more or less less less more

or more less more or less less more less or more more more less more

or less less or less more more more more more or less more less more less more or

or less less or more less less less or more more more more more more

more more or more more or less less or more less less

or less less less or more more more more

less or less more more or

or more less

more

or

or

or

or less more

or more less more less or

less more or more less or more or less

less or more or more more less or less more less or

more or less or less more or less more more less or less or more

or less more or more or less more less or less or more more less more less or

or or more more less more less or or less or less more or more

or more less more or less or more more less or less

or less more or less more less or or

more less more less more less

more or or

or

more

more

or

more less more

or less or less more more

less more more or or less or or or

or or or more less or less more or or more or

less more less or or less more more or more or or less or less

or more or more or more less or more more more less or or less more less or

or less more or or or or less or more less more more more less

more less or less or less more or less or less or

or more more more or or or less less

more or less or more more

or or less

or

or

less

or

or or or

or less or more less more

more or less or less or or more less

or or or less more less more less or or less more

less or or less more or or more less or or less or more or

or less more less more more less or less more less or less or or or or or

less or more or or less more more or less or less or less or

less more more or or or less or less or less more

less more less more less or or or or

or more more less or less

or less more

or

less

less

less

less less more

or more or or less more

less or or more less more or less more

more less or less more or more or less less more or

less less more or or more or more or more less more less or less

or more less more or or more or less more or more less more less or less or

less more or or less less more or more less more or more or less

or less more or more less less more or or less more

less more or more or or less less more

or more less more or more

less less or

less

more

more

less

less or less

more less or less less or

or or more less or more or more less

less more or or more less less or or or more or

less less less or less or or more less or more or or more or

or less more less less less more less or more less more less more less more less or

or less or less less or less less less more or less less less less

more less or or less more or more or more or more

less less or or or more less less less

less more less less more less

more or more

less

less

or

less

less less less

or more or more or more

more or less or less more less more less

less less or less more or or more less more less more

more less or less less less less less more less more or more or more

or more less more or more or more or less less less less less more less more or

less less more less more or more or more or more less less less less

more or more or less less less more or more less less

more less or less more less less more or

or or more less less more

more or less

less

or

CACOPHONY

CACAPHONY

COCAPHONY

COCOPHONY

*"Forty days of snow are
registered in the Paris archives
of 1435, the trees died and the
birds ..."*

Mais où sont les neiges d'antan? (1461 François Villon)

But where is the last yeares snow? (1653)

Tell me, if ye know; What is come of last year's snow? (1835)

Where is fled the south wind's snow? (1835)

But where are the snows of yester-year? (1869)

But where is the last year's snow? (1877)

But what has become of last year's snow? (1878)

Nay, but where is the last year's snow? (1880)

Where are the snows of yester year? (1882)

Where are the snows of a-year-agone? (1883)

Where are the snows of yesterday? (1885)

Where are the snows of long ago? (1887)

But where be the last year's Snows? (1893)

But where are the snows that were white last year? (1896)

But what is become of last year's snow? (1899)

But — where are the last year's snows? (1900)

But where indeed is last year's snow? (1900)

Where are the snows of yesteryear? (1900)

Where are the Snows of Yesterday? (1902)

But where are the winter's snows? (1905)

But where are the last year's snows? (1914)

Where are the snows that fell last year? (1917)

Who had gone like last year's snow. (1917)

But where, ah where be last year's snows? (1924)

Where are the snows of a-year-agone? (1924)

My grief for snow all gone to mist! (1924)

O, where are the snows of the years long gone? (1927)

Where are the snows of the years long gone? (1927)

But where are the snows of last year gone? (1928)

Ah, where are last winter's snows? (1930)

Canst mark the trace of last year's snow? (1934)

But where are they, the snows of yore? (1935)

But where are the snows that fell last year! (1937)

But where are the snows of other years? (1938)

But where are last year's snows? (1940)

But where is the snow that fell last year? (1946)

Where are the snows of yesteryear? (1952)

aye whaur are the snows langsyne? (1953)

Where are the snows of yesteryear? (1955)

Where are the snows of the vanished year? (1956)

But last year's snow, where has it gone? (1957)

But where are the snows of bygone years? (1960)

The snow melts, and where is it then? (1961)

Oh, where is last year's snow? (1961)

But where are last year's snows? (1961)

But where are the snows of last year? (1965)

But where are the snows of last year gone? (1968)

But where are last year's snows? (1968)

But where shall last year's snow be found? (1969)

Where, Mother of God, is last year's snow? (1973)

Whither the drift of last year's snow? (1973)

Where are the snows of yesteryear? (1975)

But then where is all of last year's snow? (1976)

Where is the drift of last year's snow? (1978)

They are now all gone like last year's snow (1979)

They are now gone from this life like last year's snow (1979)

But where are the snows of last winter? (1982)

But where are last year's snows? (1984)

But where are snows of a bygone year? (1990)

Ay, whaur's the snaws o langsyne? (1993)

Where are the snows of yesteryear? (1993)

But what's become of last year's snows? (1994)

But where are the snows of yore? (1995)

Where are yesteryear's snows? (1997)

But what's become of last year's snows? (1997)

Where are the snows of years gone by? (1999)

But where are the snows of yesteryear? (1999)

But whither have gone the snows of yore? (1999)

But then, what has become of last year's snows? (2000)

But where are the snows of yesterday? (2000)

Where are the snows of years gone by? (2000)

Oh, where is last year's snow? (2004)

Where are the snows of last winter? (2004)

Where are last year's falls of snow? (2006)

But what about the snows? (2006)

Where'd they go? (2006)

Where are the snows of vanished years? (2009)

Where are the snows like yesterday? (2010)

But where are last year's snows gone? (2011)

Well, where could last year's snows have gone? (2013)

And where is the snow that fell last year? (2013)

But where are the snows that fell last year? (2013)

O where are gone the snows of yore? (2013)

But where do they sleep, the snows of last year? (2014)

where goes snow when snow goes? (2014)

none the less
none the

CALL
MOM

a force

ray of light

spirit

the unconscious

music

air

water

a stream

a web

glue

clusters

sediment

magma flow

semen

excrement

DNA

skin

a virus

an organism

a person

wings

womb

an encyclopaedia

a house

prison

fortress

channel

a road

the city

the crust of our earth

noise

sense

a medium

a trace

a bond

currency .

technology

resource

capital

a property

commodity

material

matter

substance

a dance

a game

struggle

washing dishes

technology

a computer

radio

map

a crystal

set of pictures

a container

a hanger

toolkit

weapon

marbles

hard coin

S

TO

NRL

OG

IC

NO
K**NO**THING

rise
rise
rise
rise
rise
rise
rise
rise
rise
rise
rise
rise
rise
rise
rise
rise
rise
rise
rise
rise
rise
rise
rise
rise
rise
rise
rise
rise
rise
rise
rise
rise
rise
rise
rise
rise
rise
rise
rise
rise
rise
rise
rise
rise
rise
rise
rise

rise
rise
rise
rise
rise
rise
rise
rise
rise
rise
rise
rise
rise
rise
rise
rise
rise
rise
rise
rise
rise
rise
rise
rise
rise
rise
rise
rise
rise
rise
rise
rise
rise
rise
rise
rise
rise
rise
rise
rise
rise
rise
rise
rise
rise
rise
rise
rise
rise
rise
rise

DAY

WITHOUT

EUPHORIA

BYTHE
LIGHT
OFTHE
ANYTH
INGCA
NBURN
INTHE
FIRE
OFCO
MPL
AINT.

day out, born old

blind

as promised,

count

the days, wildebeest, sixteen

years in the dark

nothing there, either, a

three weeks' overdue

moment or two of panic

whether

it was a bright and sunny

yes, or not

the result was an instant,

after four centuries of,

still they have, after a season

of acrimony, over a years'

anxious wait,

at the time of the pre

maturely aged, talk

very slowly

the next verse began

long afterwards, which lasted circa

one night, nor one-and-a-half

minutes, round next

next so soon, for a change

the one hour, one hour, had

to have happened

seven years ago, a long-standing

date reed

for the evening

what's late and what's early,

for most of the morning

the ills of the present,

eventually must

jump, after him, minutes

watching, ways of research, a moment

before the whites came

a moment or two before, of panic

always predictable, pre

figured obligation

what should have been

promise,

after supper, as a baby

once, no more, day

out,

day

in, dimly

ripe

in the dreamtime

times of want, after

coffee

departure

temporary, descending

there came news, at mealtime

in lunchbreak,

it was time to die, after reading this text

in appearance when it appeared drunk it

was time to go, stay a bit

later faster,

a long

outwaiting at the

close of the whenever

when some lie

dormant for decades so

long as they persist,

two months late, sometime, somewhen

else, they're not young you know they're old

and if that's going to be the future

without a word

there was a moment of silence,

one year

of plenty followed by

seven years of lean might be

deprogrammed not whatever some

not for five days

mind abstracted in the

never have postulated

end of our world, yet there were times

before it rained again

in the night, in the morning again

if, one year one day at four

again, this

had happened seven

years ago, at the end of five minutes

at the time of aversion, one-day

when the grass dried

because

it was dry season

okay,

delay

was limbo

and an overcoming,

a resistance, past before-light

tire, retire, post

an hour's walk, the five days

at the time of horror, a hole

already

on the way down, done

sooner

claim back, day

out, day

FAUX **MORTS**

MOTS FORTS

MANY OF YOU
ARE SOME OF
YOU ARE **MANY**

back from the dead, or wherever the hell he'd gone

on to Mount Parnassus, Houston, Smithers

somewhere like that, bummer alert

it's a tough town to couch-surf they say

he decided to swallow his ticket

to the hereafter, I could see ghostly reflections

of the drapery, the chesterfield shimmered

when I looked in the refrigerator, I pissed

I'm so scared and everything, then I'm totally pausing

and, ah you know, really stupid uh so

she goes on about how we are all so socialized like why

palimpsest has a pimp in it, denuded

of their traditional lands and so forth, blah blah blah I never heard

of a missionary society started

by humanists or communists or atheists

or any such individuals

these verses clearly say His people

should have no dealings

with sorcery, necromancers

Koreans, Chinese, Cubans ugh

yeah then these fellas don't take baths, can you smell me that

I mean, does everything I end up touching just turn to shit or what, my kids

you know they're gonna suffer because they didn't have a father and stuff

you're dealing with people's emotions and people's psyche the

patient can be tied down

with straps, belts, bungees, a cinch

or something or other, whatever's at hand

fast-food joints and hospitals, you name it

could they *not* make a teardrop, I don't know

one recent study examined how long people watching *Mr. Bean*

at the Dentist were able to keep one hand immersed in ice-cold water

milk was used though

for the close-up of his innards, along

with pasta and glass marbles

after you find it out

it starts to look like it

it was like a Friday night kinda

anger, pain, alcoholism, sexual arousal, take your pick

I was just lying there and crap, like with my face to the wall

he slams me into the concrete the

stun effect, hallucinations, hysteria

in this world, more specifically

there's murder, rape, abuse, suicide, abortion, human sacrifice

everybody else's fame – please, on Earth

I just remember crying about being sad

lactive sickness, need, heartache, this and that

blood with cream in it, mentions

too, there was the loneliness

when I didn't have an assistant, a wardrobe girl

or anyone, I suppose

French is the language of love and stuff

evil is pain and war you know

conscience, horror, despair

all the dismal scenes of woe, no faith

in counsellors, social workers, psychiatrists, psychologists, so on

all gated communities even have a quiz

to see if you're a child molester, a spazz or pyromaniac

or anything so-and-whomsoever says

distress should never be taken superficially

or reckoned with summarily as a lack, of

misery or whatnot –

sundry apparitions warning

karma's in every bad thing coming your way, bub

including any victim status, natural devastation, ill health

people always have believed

lonely and desolate places haunted by devils

sad, strange, risky – you get it

the human foot of clay walks incautious, that dross

if only the world would *fuck* in times of stress, trauma, crush

the deathbed of hope is the cradle of despair, all the rest

when the motor's running, keep your fingers, hair, worry beads

out of the mechanism, a storyful

of dark satanic peasants, howling winds, and pigs' bladders

yes, your father was murdered by your uncle

or something or whatever

or me

look, I had work to do, defining myself as a painter

an *Eggs 'N' Things* sign, prestige and so on

just remember when you worked in the pits

factories, slums, and apartment houses, sawdust flour

bread with artificially coloured marmalade now

first they'll tease 'em, then they'll try to say they stink

like, the guano miners eventually

turned the mummy's remains over

to an agent for the Smithsonian then

they disappeared from history, extract, prick

the shoulders or any part with needles, squeeze for quotes

made trivial, rivers swapped

for trinkets, tortured in various ways

to admit the rights of Martians, animals

we'll hafta be aware of nature and the environment

whales, candlelight, and stuff like that

acid rain, radioactive waste, oil spills

bambivalent

two-headed deer

some real problems

the local garbage dump of everywhere

or anywhere and all what's in-between

bunny parts, rabbit stages, unique instants when

we go see the movie and eat popcorn and Junior Mints

or whatever the fuck else, I've seen

people that had their legs and so on amputated

unless you train in Afghanistan or Vietnam or Iraq or somewhere

love and pain are neither harder nor easier than cognition nor dozens

of people, especially younger ones, disappearing from their homes

we all want a warm place to sleep yadda yadda

just say it: you had it blocked out coz

of the severe shock, the concussion

I guess everyone felt, felt

we were older, only forced

labour, stone-age degeneracy, along with others

the first shall be last and the last shall be first

standing in for mechanised humans – work-and-sex machines

being, nothingness, death, alienation, boredom, fear, emotions,

    recognition, sympathy, empathy, shame, space-time, economic systems

                        won't mend

types of forces

contact forces, action-at-a-distance forces

general extenders, yep, you really can get high

off lip balm on your eyelids

wanna try, or what

LOOK
AWAY

ISN'T
IT NOT
IMPORT'NT?

in—out—across—away—towards—
across—away—towards—out—out—
towards—towards—in—in—in—
away—across—out—across—away—
out—in—away—towards—across—
across—in—towards—out—away—
out—away—in—in—across—
in—towards—across—towards—in—
towards—across—away—away—out—
away—out—out—across—towards—
towards—in—away—across—out—
out—towards—across—out—towards—
away—away—out—in—across—
across—out—towards—towards—in—
in—across—in—away—away—
towards—away—across—out—in—
across—out—towards—away—across—
out—in—away—towards—out—
in—across—out—across—towards—
away—towards—in—in—away—
across—in—towards—out—away—
out—away—in—away—towards—
away—across—out—in—in—
in—towards—across—towards—out—
towards—out—away—across—across—

towards-away-across-in-out-
in-out-away-towards-in-
out-across-in-across-away-
across-in-out-away-across-
away-towards-towards-out-towards-
out-in-across-away-towards-
across-away-out-towards-across-
away-out-towards-in-out-
in-across-away-across-away-
towards-towards-in-out-in-
across-away-towards-in-out-
out-across-in-away-in-
towards-towards-out-across-towards-
away-in-away-towards-away-
in-out-across-out-across-
in-towards-across-away-out-
out-out-away-across-away-
across-in-towards-out-towards-
away-across-in-in-in-
towards-away-out-towards-across-
across-towards-out-in-away-
away-away-across-out-out-
towards-in-in-away-in-
out-out-away-towards-across-
in-across-towards-across-towards-

out—in—across—towards—away—
across—across—towards—in—in—
towards—towards—out—across—across—
away—away—away—towards—out—
in—out—in—out—away—
across—in—away—out—towards—
in—across—out—towards—in—
out—away—across—away—away—
away—towards—in—in—out—
towards—out—towards—across—across—
towards—out—away—across—in—
in—across—towards—away—out—
away—towards—across—out—across—
out—in—in—towards—towards—
across—away—out—in—away—
towards—across—away—out—in—
across—out—towards—across—out—
in—towards—out—away—away—
out—away—in—in—across—
away—in—across—towards—towards—
across—towards—out—away—in—
away—out—across—in—out—
towards—away—in—towards—across—
in—across—away—out—towards—
out—in—towards—across—away—

across-in-out-away-towards-
towards-across-across-out-across-
away-out-in-in-in-
out-towards-towards-across-away-
in-away-away-towards-out-
towards-across-in-away-out-
out-in-away-in-in-
in-out-out-out-towards-
away-away-across-across-across-
across-towards-towards-towards-away-
in-out-away-towards-across-
towards-across-across-away-in-
out-towards-out-out-towards-
away-in-towards-across-away-
across-away-in-in-out-
out-towards-away-across-in-
towards-in-out-in-away-
in-out-towards-towards-out-
away-across-across-out-towards-
across-away-in-away-across-
away-across-in-towards-out-
in-in-away-in-in-
across-out-towards-out-across-
out-towards-across-across-towards-
towards-away-out-away-away-

away-towards-across-out-in-
in-in-away-towards-out-
out-out-in-in-towards-
towards-across-out-away-across-
across-away-towards-across-away-
away-out-towards-in-across-
across-in-across-across-in-
out-across-in-out-away-
towards-away-out-towards-towards-
in-towards-away-away-out-
in-away-out-towards-across-
out-towards-away-away-in-
away-out-in-in-towards-
towards-in-towards-across-away-
across-across-across-out-out-
in-across-out-away-towards-
across-out-towards-across-out-
towards-in-across-out-in-
out-towards-away-in-across-
away-away-in-towards-away-
away-towards-in-across-out-
across-in-away-out-towards-
towards-across-across-towards-across-
out-away-out-in-in-
in-out-towards-away-away-
in-out-away-towards-across-

MINIMAL
REALISTIC
PLEASURE

lately   i

find   my

self   in

the   posi   i

tion   of

comfort   t

ing   my   a

busers   .

in my eyes

in my face

in my voice

in my neck

in my throat

in my shoulders

in my heart

in my lungs

in my sternum

in my gut

in my tummy

in my legs

in my knees

in my bones

in my brain, liver

in my frontal lobe

in my lower back

in my upper chest

in my every fibre

in my eyes and cheekbones

in my neck and back

in my shoulders and back

in my chest, a tightness

in my heart and throat

in my whole bloody body

in my social organs in general

in everywhere, flushing, sweating, pounding heart

in my collarbone and neck area

in my hands, tingling or prickling sensations

in my left shoulder blade, aches and pounds

in my stomach, and my back is paining too

in my arms, my arms feel big and heavy

in my head, like my head's in a vice grip

in and around and behind my eyes and back of head

in my heart, it feels like a knife going through it

in my left arm, there's tingling and bad chest pains
and tension

in my neck and stomach, grief i feel in my chest and lungs

in nowhere, i don't feel anything in my body, more
like numb

in my skull, there's a serious crater on the upper-right
back of my skull

in my abdomen, feels like there is a wet hole into the
cold, hard air

in my feet, they become cold, i warm them, but gain no
pleasure from the warmth

in the left corner of my mouth, a string or hook or
something tugs it down, cheeks feel wet/heavy

in my whole body, this weird pain, muscle pain, pelvic
pain, dizziness, headache, shortness of breath

in my head i have tingling sensations, my palms are sweaty,
my heart is racing or pounding

in my whole body, with a lot of it (most of the anxious
part) in my guts

in my forehead, thinking about cracking it open with the black & decker cordless to let demons escape

in my stomach and throat, they ache and i feel anxious, my body aches and i feel fluish

in my entire body, but it also results in back pain, knotted muscles, sciatica, dry skin, and general achiness

in my muscles, something like worms living in my body, crawling at times to different parts of my body

in my skull, lots of migraines, stomach pains, lower-back pain, jaw is clenched and i can't relax, it sux

in my left shoulder blade, top of my head, stomach, my shoulder blade feels like something's been shoved under it

in my whole body, it becomes alien to me, it feels very
light, as if it is floating on air

in my chest my heart feels heavy, i have all this personal
baggage weighing me down, carrying around this great
big lump

in my lungs initially, like sacks of poison burst in my
upper chest, it trickles down towards my lower and side
organs

in my chest i feel a heaviness, it's always the same,
i feel so heavy and weighted down like i'm walking
through mud

in my upper stomach, lower chest, line of numbness running
from just below my brain to my mid-back and spreading
through my upper chest

in my throat and heart but it's everywhere, perhaps my
heart is broken, my whole chest feels like it's being
crushed, it's hard to breathe

in my limbs, my body seems very heavy and it's an effort
to move, tired and painful, i feel like gravity is pushing
me down

in my whole body, i physically shake while the battle
goes on inside, i get very confused and can sit for hours
battling with myself

in my chest i feel heavy and dizzy several times a day,
i feel like i'm going crazy, i am often angry and upset
for nothing

in my throat — throat freezes up and my body feels divided
from the diaphragm up, numbness and tingling throughout
the upper back, chest, and across my arms

in my stomach i feel tense, i feel like i am losing out,
i become immobilized on things because i can't make up my
mind on anything

in my throat there's a huge lump and i feel as if i'm
drowning, my husband says the light goes out in my eyes and
my eyes look dead

in my chest i feel a heaviness, and i feel like there is a
brick at the back of my neck, my back begins aching, whole
body feels tense

in my entire body, it aches and feels like it's going to
break, slow, heavy, lethargic, and painful, every morning
i wake with a sore throat, headache, and blocked nose

in my head i feel pressures, and tension in the back of
my neck, pain in my limbs, and frequent headaches, parts
of my body feel as if they don't belong to me

in my skin and muscles, a leaden heaviness,
constant exhaustion, and a sense of restriction and
tightening – the bare materiality of my body, sometimes
a literal freezing and reification, i'm incapable of
resonating with my environment

in my head, like it's stuffed full of lead, lethargic, my
legs feel heavy all the time and i feel ridiculously tired,
sometimes i feel so numb i feel like i can't eat anything or
i feel too sad to eat

in my chest, very tight, often the emotional and mental pain
is so severe it's very nearly a physical pain, i feel as
though i literally have a broken heart, massive exhaustion,
where my body won't co-operate, as though i'd been very
physically active for a long period and needed to rest

in my chest, the tip of this huge upside-down stony pyramid
weighs right down on top of my chest, the tip is rounded or
flat, it's just higher than my heart to the right a little,
maybe this is mostly anxiety, right there in the air, i try
to swipe it away with my hand, i try not to fall back from
the weight pushing

in my stomach, a horrible physical pain that is constant,
a restlessness that makes me tense up all my muscles and
writhe around, and an endless shortness of breath, it is
so bad that i am sure that i must be dying or that these
feelings must be some signal that my life is about to end —
because no one can possibly endure these feelings for any
significant amount of time

in my head, it gets in a fog and confusion is great,
physically i feel like a really bad cold, you have no
energy and feel totally drained, even the simplest of
tasks seem to take ten times the energy it normally would,
it's like walking around in lead boots, also find it hard
to regulate simple things like body temperature and u
feel permanently run down, i also find that my physical
illnesses worsen or get harder to control

in all my body, i have this energy, not a pleasant energy,
rather an uncomfortable feeling of excess, a sort of sexual
excitement but not exactly so, something electric moving in
my flesh, a current or a heat, something biting, scorching,
burning, i don't know, life itself must be like this, if
you're able to understand it or somehow control it, but for
me, the only way to cope with this energy is to masturbate
till it fades away

nature morte

натюрморт

Stillleben

静物画

bodegón

naturaleza muerta

stilleven

natürmort

ηεκρή φύση

natureza-morta

asetelma

natura morta

still life

adhuc vitam

dead nature

R U
O K

or
more
more or less
more more or or less less
more more more more or or or less less
more more more more more or or or or less less less
more more more more more more more or or or or or less less less
more more more more more more more more or or or or or or less less less less
more more more more more more more or or or or or less less less
more more more more more or or or or less less less
more more more more or or or less less
more more or or less less
more or less
more
or
or
or less more
or or less less more more
or or or or less less less more more
or or or or or less less less less more more more
or or or or or or or less less less less less more more more
or or or or or or or or less less less less less less more more more more
or or or or or or or less less less less less more more more
or or or or or less less less less more more more
or or or or less less less more more
or or less less more more
or less more
or
less
less
less more or
less less more more or or
less less less less more more more or or
less less less less less more more more more or or or
less less less less less less less more more more more more or or or
less less less less less less less less more more more more more more or or or or
less less less less less less less more more more more more or or or
less less less less less more more more more more or or or
less less less less more more more more or or
less less more more or or
less more or
less
or

Contents

Acknowledgments

Books are written by communities. I'd like to
acknowledge editorial input, content contributions
and personal support from Andrea Actis,
Dan Adleman, Brian Ang, Sean Arden, Kate Armstrong,
Michael Barnholden, Rachel Eden Baumann,
Jordan Bent, Gregory Betts, Lindsey Boldt, Mike Borkent,
Jamey Braden, Lary Bremner, Rebecca Brewer,
Brandon Brown, David Buuck, Ted Byrne, Louis Cabri,
Steve Calvert, Tommy Chain, Fabiola Carranza,
Scott Cohen, Steve Collis, Wayde Compton,
Peter Culley, Mark Dahl, Jeff Derksen, Craig Dworkin,
Scott Elwood, Jeneen Frei Njootli, Colin Fulton,
Aurelio Giardini, Janet Giltrow, Aaron Griggs,
Shazia Hafiz Ramji, Eli Horn, Chris Hutchinson,
Megan Hepburn, Stacey Ho, Scott Inniss,
Anahita Jamali Rad, Am Johal, Reg Johanson,
Shallom Johnson, Andreas Kahre, Amy Kazymerchyk,
Trish Klein, Kevin Killian, Zoe Kreye,
Vanessa Kwan, Danielle LaFrance, Greg Lainsbury,
Sasha Langford, Mat Laporte, Mike Leyne,
Dorothy Trujillo Lusk, Jaleh Mansoor, Lauren Marsden,
Nicole Markotic, Rolf Maurer, Reid McFarlane,
Jay MillAr, Joe Milutis, Robert Mittenthal,
Gustave Morin, Joseph Mosconi, Alexander Muir,
Michael Nardone, Christopher Nealon, Cecily Nicholson,
Jem Noble, Sean O'Brien, Guinevere Pencarrick,

Nicholas Perrin, Chris Piuma, Spark Pylon, Brian Reed,
Ted Rees, Jamie Reid, Nikki Reimer, Aja Rose Bond,
Gabriel Saloman, Jenny Sampirisi, Alex Scott, Cam Scott,
Jordan Scott, Erin Siddall, Robin Simpson, Colin Smith,
Jeremy Stewart, Catriona Strang, Marie-Hélène Tessier,
Steven Tong, Mark Truscott, Jeremy Turner,
Nico Vassilakis, Alli Warren, James Whitman,
Sarah Whittam, Tyrone Williams, Elizabeth Williamson,
Meghan Whyte, David Wolach, Derek Woods,
Cornelia Wyngaarden, Stephanie Young, Maged Zaher.

Further thanks to everyone who helped me, hosted me,
listened to me, while I was running around (through
Montreal, Burlington, Hamilton, Toronto, Windsor,
New York, Washington, D.C., Prince George, Victoria,
Vancouver, Oakland, Portland, Olympia, Seattle) in
2014–2015 with my book *Loitersack* (New Star, 2014).
Limitless thanks to the many more friends who keep
me alive with their love, acceptance, and patience. Huge
gratitude to everyone I worked with at Talonbooks, but
especially to Les Smith and Kevin Williams.

Some of these poems were published (in different
versions) by Eth Press / Punctum Books, Malaspina
Printmaker's Society (through *Institutions by Artists*),
and CSA Space. Others were published in *Avant-Canada,
The Capilano Review, Dreamboat, Dreamland,
Generations, Laugh Zine,* and *Tripwire.*

Notes

"welcome"

> Greetings and welcomes are given here in a range
> of languages, all of which represent populations
> currently at war or under siege. The poem includes
> at least one language from each large family of
> Indigenous languages in North America: Algic,
> Iroquoian, Muskogean, Siouan, Uto-Aztecan,
> Athabaskan, Salishan, Aleut, and Mayan. It ends
> with English and Latin in order to underscore the
> colonial-imperialist and capitalist-neoliberal nature
> of these conflicts, not to privilege those languages.

"Self-Sufficient"

> Each of these arguments is "rhetorically self-
> sufficient," in that "they appeal to common sense
> and taken-for-granted value orientations" (Shiao-
> Yun Chiang) in a way that makes them challenging
> to answer on their own (semantic) terms. Most
> are commonly used to mitigate or sustain racist
> discourse. The initial fourteen examples (not in
> order of appearance) were compiled from articles by
> Martha Augoustinos and Brianne Hastie; Martha
> Augoustinos, Amanda Lecouteur, and John Soyland;
> Michael Billig; Margaret Wetherell and Jonathan
> Potter; Shiao-Yun Chiang. The rest came from my
> own reading, research, and listening.

"Bottom of the Pot"

> A poem compiled from prison, prisoner-of-war camp, concentration camp, gulag, Holocaust, and poverty soup-kitchen memoirs, spanning historically from the United States Civil War through the Bosnian genocide. The earliest version of "Bottom of the Pot," sparked by the famous passage in Primo Levi about camp inmates' competition to get their soup from the "bottom of the vat," was composed in 2005. It was intended for inclusion in *Buffet World* (New Star, 2011). I revisited, extensively revised, and expanded the piece in 2015–2016. Note that my own family was directly affected by the Holocaust. Donato Mancini, my paternal grandfather, was pressured into exile for hiding a Jewish family threatened with deportation during the last years of the war. He was compelled to emigrate with his own family from one of the most verdant, sunny regions of the planet (Abruzzo, Italy), to become a coal miner in lowland Belgium (in the village of Havré in the province of Hainaut), where he would die of the lung cancer induced by coal dust. I hope the poem will be read as the traumatic recollection it is for me, equally an anti-prison and anti-war poem, broaching core issues of arbitrary power, unearned privilege, poverty, and abjection.

"Snowline"

> This poem compiles translations of François Villon's famous line: "Mais où sont les neiges d'antan?" (1461). Most are from complete translations of the untitled source poem, conventionally referred to as "Ballade des dames du temps jadis." See, for comparison, Caroline Bergvall's poem "VIA (48 Dante Variations)."

"Langue Analog"

> A curated collection of analogies used to explain what language is. Language itself is said to be like each of these things.

"day out, born old"

> Every clause in this poem turns on a deictic marker for time. Like many poems in *Same Diff*, it attempts to overcome the limitations of verb-tense in English to evoke a sensation of non-colonial, non-capitalist time as polyvalent, spherical, and simultaneous. To affect a "tidalectic" (Kamau Brathwaite) macro rhythm, the clauses were arranged by length: increasing-decreasing-increasing-decreasing.

"whales, candlelight, and stuff like that"

    The title (and title-line) of this poem are drawn from
Maryann Overstreet's book *Whales, Candlelight,
and Stuff Like That: General Extenders in English
Discourse* (2000). Much of the original material –
utterances ending with a "general extender" (and so
on; stuff like that; etcetera) – was gathered online,
from print sources, or by eavesdropping. The rest
was invented.

"Where do you feel?"

    A poem of answers to the question "Where in
your body do you feel grief, anxiety, and/or
depression?" collected from social media, print, and
personal sources. Deepest thanks to everyone who
contributed. Several of the answers are my own.

Sources

"Bottom of the Pot"

Aida, Yūji. *Prisoner of the British: A Japanese Soldier's Experiences in Burma* (1966).

Applebaum, Anne. *Gulag: A History* (2003).

——, ed. *Gulag Voices: An Anthology* (2012).

Beevor, Antony. *Stalingrad* (1998).

Ben-Atar, Roma Nutkiewicz, and Doron S. Ben-Atar. *What Time and Sadness Spared: Mother and Son Confront the Holocaust* (2006).

Berkman, Alexander. *Prison Memoirs of an Anarchist* (1912).

Boyd, Belle. *Belle Boyd in Camp and Prison* (1865).

Brandt, Anthony. *The Man Who Ate His Boots: The Tragic History of the Search for the Northwest Passage* (2008).

Chester, Robert. "On the Bottom." Rev. of *If This Is a Man [Survival in Auschwitz]* by Primo Levi. *International Socialist Review* 21.3: 94 (1960).

Christ, Roxane. *I Am (Not) a Hero, I Am a Survivor: The Story of Lou Van Coevorden* (2004).

Ciszek, Fr. Walter, S.J. *With God in Russia* (1964).

Cronk Farrell, Mary. *Pure Grit: How American World War II Nurses Survived Battle and Prison Camp* (2014).

Dyer, Frederick Henry. *A Compendium of the War of the Rebellion* (1908).

Eliach, Yaffa. *Hasidic Tales of the Holocaust* (1982).

Frankl, Viktor E. *Man's Search for Meaning* (1946).

Gammon, Carolyn, and Christiane Hemker. *Johanna Krause Twice Persecuted: Surviving in Nazi Germany and Communist East Germany* (2007).

Gayler, Robert. *Private Prisoner: An Astonishing Story of Survival Under the Nazis* (1984).

Geve, Thomas. *Guns and Barbed Wire: A Child Survives the Holocaust* (1987).

Gilliland, Betty June. *Destiny's Tapestry* (2014).

Gutowski, Gene. *With Balls and Chutzpah: A Story of Survival* (2003).

Gyaw, Htun Aung. "Burma's Insein Prison: Punishment and Oppression." *Crime, Law, and Social Change* 15.2: 125–34 (1991).

Hammerschlag, Dr. Carl A. "Ella's Story." *Healing Doc.* February 5. Web. (2006).

Hawkins, Christopher. *The Adventures of Christopher Hawkins* (1864).

Hitchcock, George A. *"Death does seem to have all he can attend to": The Civil War Diary of an Andersonville Survivor* (1865).

Huener, Jonathan. *Auschwitz, Poland, and the Politics of Commemoration, 1945–1979* (2003).

Izetbegović, Alija. *Izetbegović of Bosnia-Herzegovina: Notes from Prison, 1983–1988* (2002).

Karay, Felicja. *Death Comes in Yellow* (1996).

Klainman, Jorge I. *The Seventh Miracle* (2000).

Klein, Jill G. "Calories for Dignity: Fashion in the Concentration Camp." *Advances in Consumer Research* 30.1: 34 (2003).

Kok-Schurgers, G. Pauline. *The Remains of War: Surviving the Other Concentration Camps of World War II* (2011).

Krammer, Arnold. *Prisoners of War: A Reference Handbook* (2007).

Levi, Primo. *Survival in Auschwitz* [U.S. edition of *If This Is a Man*] (1947).

Liberation: An Independent Monthly, Volumes 1–4 (1956).

Maile, John Levi. *Prison Life in Andersonville* (1912).

McDougall, William H. *By Eastern Windows: The Story of a Battle of Souls and Minds in the Prison Camps of Sumatra* (1949).

McElroy, John. *Andersonville: A Story of Rebel Military Prisons* (1879).

Mckellar, Robert. *Target of Opportunity and Other War Stories* (2011).

Mishell, William W. *Kaddish for Kovno: Life and Death in a Lithuanian Ghetto, 1941–1945* (1988).

Mózes, Teréz. *Staying Human Through the Holocaust* (2005).

Nathan, Joan. *The Foods of Israel Today* (2001).

Neave, Denny, and Craig Edwin Smith. *Aussie Soldier Prisoners of War* (2009).

Ó Gráda, Cormac. *Eating People Is Wrong, and Other Essays on Famine, Its Past, and Its Future* (2015).

O'Hare, Kate Richards. *In Prison* (1923).

Pickenpaugh, Roger. *Captives in Blue: The Civil War Prisons of the Confederacy* (2013).

Piotrowski, Tadeusz. *The Polish Deportees of World War II: Recollections of Removal to the Soviet Union and Dispersal Throughout the World* (2004).

Ranasinghe, Anne. *At What Dark Point* (1991).

Rochlitz, Imre, and Joseph Rochlitz. *Accident of Fate: A Personal Account, 1938–1945* (2011).

Saidel, Rochelle G. *The Jewish Women of Ravensbrück Concentration Camp* (2004).

Shalamov, Varlam. *Kolyma Tales* (1978).

Sherwin, Byron L., and Susan G. Ament. *Encountering the Holocaust: An Interdisciplinary Survey* (1979).

Sofsky, Wolfgang. *The Order of Terror: The Concentration Camp* (1997).

Solzhenitsyn, Alexander. *One Day in the Life of Ivan Denisovich* (1962).

Soumerai, Eve Nussbaum, and Carol D. Schulz. *Daily Life During the Holocaust* (1998).

Speer, Lonnie R. *Portals to Hell: Military Prisons of the Civil War* (1997).

Springfield-Greene Country Library System. "Colvin, William & John." *Trans-Mississippi Theater Photo Archive*. Web. (2013).

Tabori, George. *The Cannibals* (1968).

Tenenbaum, Joseph E. *Legacy and Redemption: A Life Renewed* (2006).

Terkel, Studs. *Hard Times: An Oral History of the Great Depression* (1970).

Thomson, Ian. *Primo Levi: A Life* (2003).

Thurow, Roger, and Scott Kilman. *Enough: Why the World's Poorest Starve in an Age of Plenty* (2010).

Topolski, Aleksander. *Without Vodka: Wartime Adventures in Russia* (1999).

Turtledove, Harry. *Walk in Hell: The Great War, Book Two* (1999).

Vallgren, Carl-Johan. *Documents Concerning Rubashov the Gambler* (1996).

Wachsmann, Nikolaus. *KL: A History of the Nazi Concentration Camps* (2015).

Walcott, Charles Folsom. *History of the Twenty-first Regiment, Massachusetts Volunteers, in the War for the Preservation of the Union, 1861–1865: With Statistics of the War and of Rebel Prisons* (1882).

Walsh, Edmund Aloysius. *The Last Stand: An Interpretation of the Soviet Five-Year Plan* (1931).

Weingartner, Steven, ed. *A Weekend with the Great War:* Proceedings of the Fourth Annual Great War Interconference Seminar, Lisle, Illinois, September 16–18 (1994).

Wiernicki, John. *War in the Shadow of Auschwitz: Memoirs of a Polish Resistance Fighter and Survivor of the Death Camps* (2001).

Yudelevitch, Dovid. *In Every Generation: The Life and Legacy of the Gaon and Tzaddik Rav Shmuel Aharon Yudelevitch, zt"l* (2004).

"Snowline"

Epigraph: Henry De Vere Stacpoole

Translators, by year (repetitions are intentional)

(1653) Thomas Urquhart
    (via François Rabelais)
(1835) Henry Francis Cary
(1835) Louisa Stuart Costello
(1869) Dante Gabriel Rossetti
(1877) Walter Besant (via Rabelais)
(1878) John Payne
(1880) Andrew Lang
(1882) Robert Louis Stevenson
    (via Rossetti)
(1883) Charles Kegan Paul
(1885) W.R. Willis
(1887) Stephen Decatur Smith, Jr.
(1893) William Francis Smith
    (via Rabelais)
(1896) Leonard Doughty
(1899) John Payne
(1900) Henry Carrington
(1900) J.J. Ellis
(1900) J.J. Ellis (via Rossetti)
(1902) George Moorehead
(1905) Emma Kate Armstrong
(1914) Henry De Vere Stacpoole
(1917) Paul Hookham
(1917) Arthur Symons
(1924) John Heron Lepper
(1924) George Heyer
(1924) Michael Scot
(1927) Herbert Edward Palmer

(1927) Herbert Edward Palmer
(1928) J.U. Nicolson
(1930) Geoffroy Atkinson
(1934) N. Scarlyn Wilson
(1935) Lewis Wharton
(1937) John Erskine
(1938) Ralph Nixon Currey
(1940) Edward F. Chaney
(1946) Harry Bertram McCaskie
(1952) Norman Cameron
(1953) Tom Scott
(1955) George Peddy Cuttino
(1956) S.A. DeWitt
(1957) J.M. Synge
(1960) Anthony Bonner
(1961) Gerhard Nellhaus
    (via Bertolt Brecht)
(1961) Robert Lowell
(1961) Brian Woledge
(1965) Galway Kinnell
(1968) Beram Saklatvala
(1968) Robert Anacker
(1969) Richard Wilbur
(1973) Robert Lowell
(1973) Peter Dale
(1975) Anthony Weir
(1976) Stephen Rodefer
(1978) Peter Dale
(1979) Arpad Barna

(1979) Arpad Barna

(1982) Galway Kinnell

(1984) John Fox

(1990) John Frederick Nims

(1993) Tom Scott

(1993) Robin Shirley

(1994) Barbara N. Sargent-Baur

(1995) Louis Filler
(via Stephenson)

(1997) Gregory Orr

(1997) David A. Fein

(1999) Ken Knabb

(1999) Ken Knabb

(1999) Marcel Kopp

(2000) Michael Freeman

(2000) Louis Aston Marantz Simpson

(2000) Aubrey Burl

(2004) A.S. Kline

(2004) Stephen Eridan

(2006) Martin Sorrell

(2006) Michael Freeman

(2006) Martin Sorrell

(2009) Justin Clemens

(2010) Alfred Colo

(2011) David Yendley

(2013) A.Z. Foreman

(2013) David Georgi

(2013) Anthony Mortimer

(2013) Florence Dujarric

(2014) Donato Mancini
(via Attilio Carminati)

(2014) Michael Barnholden

Talonbooks
278 East First Avenue, Vancouver, British Columbia, Canada V5T 1A6
www.talonbooks.com

First printing: 2017

Typeset in Century Schoolbook Mono and Roboto Sans
Printed and bound in Canada on 100% post-consumer recycled paper

Interior and cover design by Donato Mancini and Typesmith
Cover illustration by Donato Mancini

Talonbooks acknowledges the financial support of the Canada Council for the Arts, the Government of Canada through the Canada Book Fund, and the Province of British Columbia through the British Columbia Arts Council and the Book Publishing Tax Credit.

Library and Archives Canada Cataloguing in Publication

Mancini, Donato, author
        Same diff / by Donato Mancini.

Poems.
ISBN 978-1-77201-136-4 (softcover)

        I. Title.

PS8576.A53756S26 2017   C811'.6   C2017-900722-X

A poet, visual artist, and cultural critic, Donato Mancini is the author of numerous books. These include *Ligatures* (2005), *Æthel* (2007), *Buffet World* (2011), *Fact 'n' Value* (2011), and *Loitersack* (2014). Critical writings are collected in *You Must Work Harder to Write Poetry of Excellence* (2012) and *Anamnesia: Unforgetting* (2013). Born on the traditional territory of the Haudenosaunee and Anishinaabeg, since 2001 he has lived not too far from X̱wáyx̱way, on the traditional territories of the xʷməθkwəy̓əm, Skwxwú7mesh, Stó:lō, and Səl̓ílwəta?ɬ peoples.

diff
same

same

same

diff

same

same

diff

same

diff

diff

diff

diff

same

same

diff

same

same

same

same

same

diff

same

diff

same

diff

diff

same

diff

diff

diff

same

diff

same

same

diff

same

diff

diff

same

same

diff

diff

same

same

same

same

diff

diff

same

same

diff

diff

diff

diff

diff

same

same

diff

same

same

same

same

same

diff

diff

same

diff

same

diff

diff

diff

diff

same

diff

diff